ROMAN BRITAIN

ROMAN BRITAIN
English Equivalents of Roman Place Names
1 EXETER, 2 DORCHESTER, 3 ILCHESTER,
4 WINCHESTER, 5 PORTCHESTER, 6 CHICHESTER,
7 PEVENSEY, 8 LYMPNE, 9 DOVER, 10 RICHBOROUGH,
11 RECULVER, 12 CANTERBURY, 13 ROCHESTER,
14 LONDON, 15 CHELMSFORD, 16 BRADWELL,
17 COLCHESTER, 18 ST. ALBANS, 19 SILCHESTER,
20 CIRENCESTER, 21 BATH, 22 GLOUCESTER,
23 WESTON UNDER PENYARD, 24 CAERWENT,
25 CAERLEON, 26 NEATH, 27 CARMARTHEN,
28 Y GAER, 29 LLANIO, 30 KENCHESTER,
31 CAER SWS, 32 WROXETER, 33 WALL (STAFFS.)
34 DROITWICH, 35 TOWCESTER, 36 LEICESTER,
37 WATER NEWTON (HUNTS) 38 CAISTER,
39 BURGH CASTLE, 40 BRANCASTER, 41 LINCOLN,
42 BUXTON, 43 CHESTER, 44 CAERHUN,
45 CAERNARVON, 46 ANGLESEY,
47 MANCHESTER, 48 DONCASTER,
49 BROUGH, 50 MALTON, 51 YORK,
52 ALDBOROUGH, 53 CATTERICK,
54 RAVENGLASS, 55 CARLISLE,
56 CORBRIDGE, 57 S.TH SHIELDS,
58 HIGH ROCHESTER,
59 NEWSTEAD,
60 INCHTUTHIL,
61 BOULOGNE.
Towns
Fortresses, forts
Signal Stations
Roads
PINNATA CASTRA 60
ANTONINE WALL
TRIMONTIUM 59
BREMENIUM 58
HADRIAN'S WALL
57 ARBEIA
56 CORSTOPITUM
55 LUGUVALIUM
GLANNAVENTA 54
CATARACTONIUM 53
DERVENTIO 50
ISURIUM 52
51 EBURACUM COLONIA LEG.VI
PETUARIA 49
MAMUCIUM 47
DANUM 48
46 MONA
AQUAE ARNEMETIAE 42
LINDUM COLONIA 41
CANOVIUM 44
DEVA LEG.XX 43
SEGONTIUM 45
BRANODUNUM 40
GARIANNONUM 39
32 VIROCONIUM
LETOCETUM 33
RATAE 36
DUROBRIVAE 37
VENTA ICENORUM 38
31 MEDIOMANUM
BREMIA 29
SALINAE 34
LACTODORUM 35
30 MAGNIS
28 CICUTIO
CAMULODUNUM COLONIA 17
MARIDUNUM 27
23 ARICONIUM
22 GLEVUM COLONIA
CAESAROMAGUS 15
OTHONA 16
NIDUM 26
25 ISCA LEGIONIS LEG. II
24 VENTA SILURUM
20 CORINIUM
VERULAMIUM 18
LONDINIUM 14
11 REGULBIUM
21 AQUAE SULIS
CALLEVA 19
DUROBRIVAE 13
RUTUPIAE 10
DUROVERNUM 12
9 PORTUS DUBRIS
PORTUS LEMANIS 8
VENTA BELGARUM 4
3 LINDINIS
PORTUS ADURNI 5
NOVIOMAGUS 6
7 ANDERIDA
2 DURNOVARIA
ISCA DUMNONIORUM 1
GESORIACUM 61
SCALE
20 10 0 20 40 60 80 100
MILES

ROMAN BRITAIN

Text by AILEEN FOX

Drawings by ALAN SORRELL

LUTTERWORTH PRESS · LONDON

First Published 1961
Second Impression 1962
Third Impression 1965
Fourth Impression 1966
Fifth Impression 1968
Sixth Impression 1970

The drawing by Alan Sorrell on the jacket is the property of the Ministry of Public Building and Works and is reproduced with their permission. It is Crown Copyright.
The illustrations on pages 11, 28, 41 and 45 are based on drawings by Alan Sorrell published in *The Illustrated London News*, and are reproduced by courtesy of the Editor.
The drawings on pages 16, 17, 25 and 29 are based on drawings by Alan Sorrell in the National Museum of Wales.

7188 0800 2

PRINTED IN GREAT BRITAIN BY
LOWE AND BRYDONE (PRINTERS) LTD LONDON

CONTENTS

BOOK LIST	6
THE BRITONS	7
THE CONQUEST	10
ROAD MAKING	13
THE ROMAN ARMY OF OCCUPATION	14
THE SCHEME OF GOVERNMENT	19
HADRIAN'S WALL	21
TOWNS AND TOWN LIFE	24
AMUSEMENTS	26
BUILDING CRAFTS AND TECHNIQUES	30
COUNTRY LIFE	30
DAILY LIFE	34
MINING AND METAL WORKING	36
POTTERY MAKING	38
RELIGION	40
THE END OF ROMAN BRITAIN	44
PAST AND PRESENT	48

The cover drawing shows Hadrian's Wall, looking east towards Walltown Gap, with a milecastle, turrets, the Military Way, and the mounds and ditch of the Vallum. This section of the Wall has recently been excavated and conserved by the Ministry of Public Building and Works.

SOME OTHER BOOKS ABOUT ROMAN BRITAIN

R. G. Collingwood, *Roman Britain* (Methuen 1932, out of print, but in most public libraries) and Anthony Birley, *Life in Roman Britain* (Batsford 1964) are the best books to read after this one.

I. A. Richmond, *Roman Britain* (Pelican 1963) and A. L. Rivet, *Town and Country in Roman Britain* (Hutchinson 1958) are recent authoritative historical works. Both have a full bibliography.

There are illustrations of sculpture, weapons, jewellery, pottery and other Roman things found in Britain in *Guide to Roman Britain*, published by the British Museum, and in *London in Roman Times*, published by the London Museum, Kensington Palace.

Graham Webster, *The Roman Army*, published by the Grosvenor Museum, Chester (1956) is a short book about the soldiers. There is a *Handbook to the Roman Wall* by J. Collingwood Bruce, edited by I. A. Richmond (Reid 1957), and a detailed map published by the Ordnance Survey, on the scale of 2 ins. to the mile (1964).

R. G. Collingwood, *Archaeology of Roman Britain* (Methuen 1930) and J. Ward, *Romano-British Buildings and Earthworks* (Methuen 1911) both out of print, are general well illustrated books that could also be seen in a public library.

The *Map of Roman Britain* (3rd edition 1956) published by the Ordnance Survey is very useful for finding out what Roman sites there are in any part of the country and for the names of towns and other settlements in Roman times.

If you want to find out more about Roman Britain go to the nearest museum and ask to see the Roman antiquities that have been found in your neighbourhood. It would be a good idea to visit some of the places, too, which you can find marked on the Ordnance Survey maps.

1. *The Britons: A Celtic warrior in his chariot with a driver. The chariot has a wooden frame with sides of wicker-work, the wheels have iron tyres and hub-bands. There is a bronze knob at the back for the warrior to grasp when he was getting in. In the background is the gateway to a hill-fort.*

THE BRITONS

BEFORE the Romans came, Britain was inhabited by Celtic peoples, who lived as separate tribal groups, each with a kingdom in a different part of the country. They were not a savage or backward people, but the equal in civilisation of any folk living north of the Alps in the 1st century B.C. They were skilled metal workers, using iron for their everyday tools and weapons, and bronze for their finest possessions such as the chieftain's shield and helmet, or the lady's brooch or decorated mirror. They lived in round huts

2. *Caesar's landing: A general* (legatus legionis) *is questioning a British prisoner through an interpreter: behind him is a standard bearer* (signifer) *wearing his bear-skin hood. In the background is a large marching camp with the tents for the whole army, and the ships and transports at anchor or drawn up on the beach.*

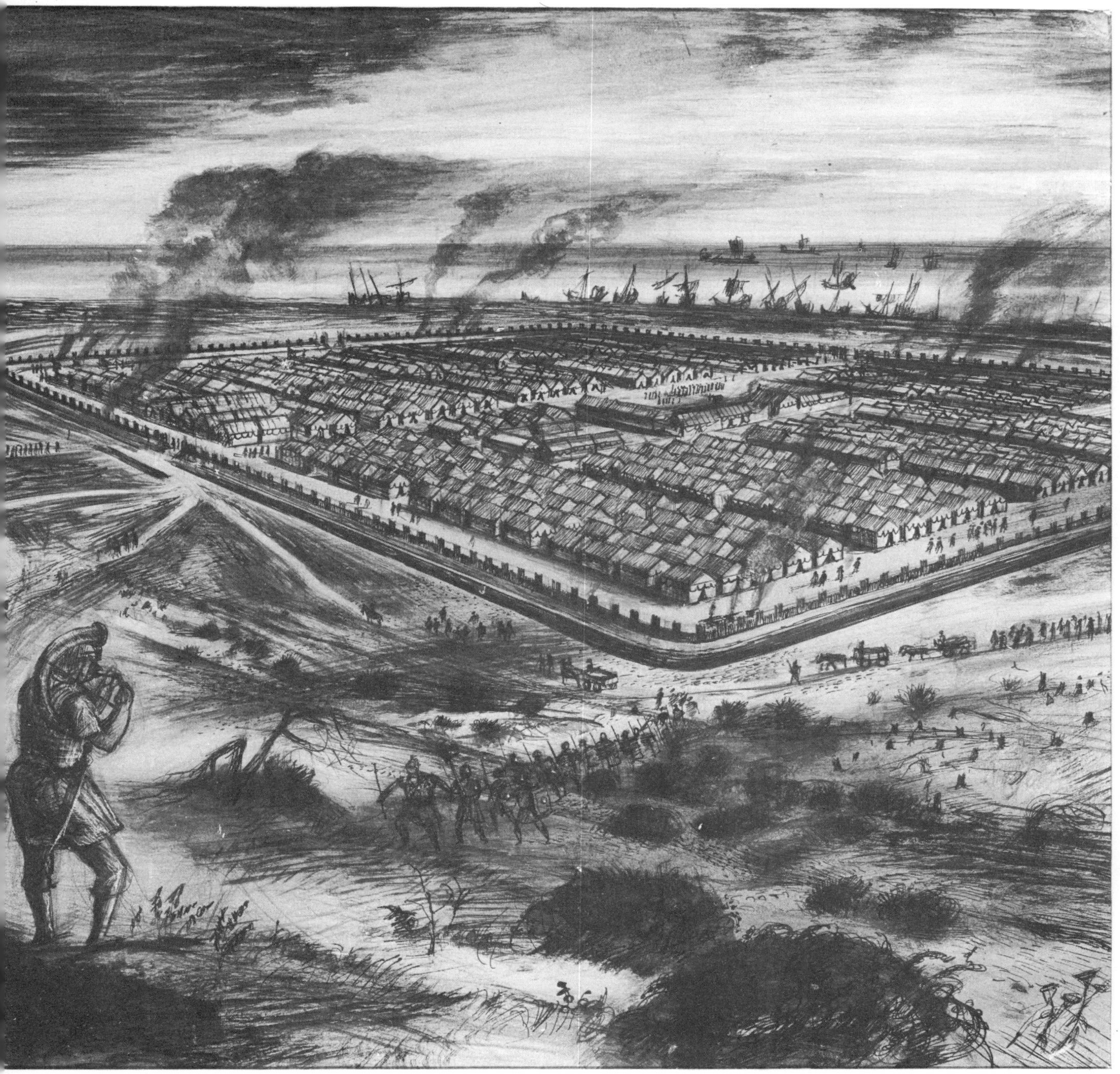

built either of wood or unmortared stone, sometimes in small homesteads, more often in a regular hilltop settlement defended by ramparts and ditches, known to the Romans as an *oppidum* and to us as a hill-fort or camp (fig. 4). The people grew corn in small square fields and reared cattle for their livelihood.

Each small tribe was ruled by a chieftain, each kingdom by a King or Queen, some of whom issued coins bearing their names, like King Cunobelin (Cymbeline), ruler of the Catuvellaunian tribes in south-eastern England.

The Celtic peoples were often at war with each other. Their warriors, who delighted in fighting, were armed with long iron slashing swords and heavy spears. They were driven into battle in light wooden chariots pulled by two ponies yoked together to a central shaft (fig. 1).

The story of Roman Britain tells how this country was conquered and then for nearly 400 years became part of the Roman Empire; and how these people soon became its willing citizens, the Roman-Britons, retaining some of their own customs but progressing in many things by adopting the Roman way of life.

THE CONQUEST

3. *The Emperor Vespasian.*

It was Julius Caesar who took the first steps to conquer Britain. He had already added the province of Gaul (modern France and Belgium) to the Roman Republic, and had then found that the Britons sent help across the Channel to the Gauls to resist him: for the Celts in Britain were of the same race as the Celts in Gaul, and various tribes had emigrated from France to settle in Britain at different times during the second and first centuries B.C.

4. *The Roman attack on Maiden Castle: The hill-fort has three large ramparts and ditches with a palisade on the crest of the innermost bank: it was entered by double gateways at either end of the mile-long enclosure, which were screened by short lengths of the outer ramparts. The Roman storming party have set fire to the cornfields outside the hill-fort to conceal the advance of the troops on the right: the catapults are in action.*

Caesar's first attempt in the year 55 B.C. was little more than a raid, because he was forced to go back when his ships were badly damaged by the September gales. The next year he sailed with five legions and two thousand cavalry from the Roman port at Boulogne, up-channel past the white chalk cliffs, and anchored off an open beach beyond the South Foreland. Here he landed; according to custom the soldiers dug a ditch and heaped up the sods and earth to make the rampart for their camp, with a palisade of stakes on top. Each unit pitched their rows of leather tents in order; headquarters at the general's tent was in the centre of the enclosure (fig. 2). The horses were picketed, stores and equipment landed. Some prisoners were brought in, from whom Caesar learned where the British forces were, under their leader Cassivellaunus.

In a series of battles he defeated the Britons, despite their clever manoeuvres with their chariots and their harassing guerilla tactics, and led the Roman army across the Thames to capture the *oppidum* of Cassivellaunus probably at Wheathampstead in Hertfordshire. Caesar then returned to Gaul, and although Britain paid tribute, and traded with the Roman world, it was nearly ninety years before the Romans again attacked.

In A.D. 43 the Emperor Claudius sent an expeditionary force led by Aulus Plautius, one of his best generals; a landing was easily effected at Richborough in Kent, commanding a safe harbour in the Wensum channel. The Britons were defeated in a battle on the river Medway and the Emperor came himself to make a triumphant entry into Camulodunum, the capital of King Cunobelin at Colchester. Most of the tribes of the south and east then submitted. Claudius went back to Rome, leaving his general as the first governor of the new province of Britannia.

The west and the north of Britain had yet to be conquered, and the Roman army was divided into three, one part going north, one north-west and one south-west. Let us follow the southern army group, which included the legion known as the Second Augustan, under the command of a young man, the future Emperor Vespasian (A.D. 69-79, fig. 3). The Celtic peoples in the south-west had many strong hill-forts, among which was the chief citadel of the group of tribes called the Durotriges, at Maiden Castle, near Dorchester. This was one of the twenty *oppida* that are recorded to have fallen to the Roman attack.

Excavations have shown that the legion attacked at the east gate (fig. 4), with a hail of iron-tipped arrows shot from machines called *ballistae,* a sort of heavy catapult which could be moved about on a wagon. The Britons slung stones from the top of the great ramparts and from platforms they had set up to command the entrance passage, winding between the steep banks and ditches. The legionaries would lock their shields together above their heads to protect themselves, like a tortoise under his shell, as they advanced. They set fire to some huts in front of the main double gateways, and broke down the doors, probably with an iron-headed battering-ram. Then a great slaughter took place, in which men, women and children were killed. Later the Britons were allowed to bury their dead, hurriedly, in front of the gate. The gates of Maiden Castle were pulled down by the soldiers before they went further on their campaign. At some hill-forts a small contingent was left behind to police the district, as at Hod Hill, near Blandford in Dorset.

The Second Augustan legion went as far west as Seaton in Devon, then they linked up north-eastwards with other forces in the Midlands and in Lincolnshire. It took the Romans in this way only three or four years to conquer the south-eastern half of England; it took them another thirty years to subdue thoroughly Wales and Yorkshire; after two attempts (A.D. 80-100 and A.D. 140-180) they abandoned the attack on Scotland. Campaigning in the hill country of the west and north proved much more difficult than in the English lowlands.

ROAD MAKING

The rapid advance of the armies was possible because the troops made good firm roads along which supplies and reinforcements could be moved quickly. Hitherto the only roads in Britain were winding trackways, which had to follow the ridges and so avoid the wooded slopes and marshy ground in the valleys. The Romans were practical road engineers, able to deal with such natural obstacles, and so they could make their roads straight across the country. The first roads in Britain were made by the army for their movements and supplies.

First the surveyors set out the line for the road, clearing the woodland in order to sight, with poles, a straight line to a point on the sky-line (fig. 5). The turf was then usually cleared off for the full width of the road, about 15 to 20 feet; a good foundation of rough stones was laid on the sub-soil, and finally a layer of gravel to make a smooth surface. The centre of the road was raised and cambered so that the rain would run off it quickly, and small ditches were often dug at either side at a short distance away to help to drain the ground.

In some places the road was raised on an embankment (*agger*), in others it was in a cutting or terraced along a hillside. There were zig-zags to ease the gradients on steep hills; the rivers were crossed on bridges, and milestones, with the Emperor's name, were put up at the roadside to show the distance to or from the nearest post. Occasionally in the hill country the road had a paved surface, and on Blackstone Edge in the Pennines a deep channel worn in the centre can still be seen where the brake-poles were put on to the carts to slow them down the hill.

The roads in the lowlands radiated from London (see frontispiece); after the conquest they served civilians and soldiers alike. Along them travellers and recruits, merchants with their wares and country folk with their produce in carts and waggons or on pack-ponies, the Governor's messengers and the vehicles of the Imperial Post to Rome moved safely and rapidly.

THE ROMAN ARMY OF OCCUPATION

After the campaigns were over a permanent army of occupation remained in the north and west of Britain, numbering about 56,000 men. There were two main classes of troops in the Roman army, the legionaries and the auxiliaries. The legions were infantry regiments 5000-6000 strong, the auxilia were units of 500 or 1000 men, either infantry or cavalry or a mixture of both. The legionaries were volunteers from men who were citizens of the Roman Empire by birth, the auxiliaries were conscripts from natives in the provinces.

The legionary enlisted for twenty years; after that he retired as a veteran, with a pension and sometimes a grant of land. His uniform consisted of a coloured leather tunic, shorts or kilt, a cuirass, usually made up of strips of bronze fastening in front, a bronze-plated leather belt from which his short iron sword (*gladius*) and dagger were hung, and a bronze helmet, which had a neckguard and ear-flaps, and on top of which a plume of horsehair could be fixed on great occasions (fig. 2). He carried a long shield

5. Road-making: The legionaries are making a road with the help of the British prisoners: the surveyor in the foreground is using a groma, *an instrument like a cross-staff for sighting at right angles. A fire has been lit far ahead to show the line of the road.*

curved to protect his body, and a *pilum,* a sort of javelin the shaft of which bent when it hit its mark, and was difficult to pull out again. On the march the legionary carried an axe, a trenching tool, and other camping kit.

In front of the columns of marching men, a gilt eagle was carried on a pole, the sacred emblem of the legion. Standard-bearers in their bear-skin hoods followed, carrying the *signa* (fig. 2), a row of medallions mounted on a pointed shaft, symbolising battle honours, which together with trumpet blasts were used to signal manoeuvres, and as rallying points in battle.

In Britain there were permanent quarters for three legions the greater part of the time, at Caerleon-on-Usk (*Isca*), at Chester (*Deva*), and at York (*Eboracum*). Each was a large rectangular fortress defended by a broad ditch and a rampart. A stone wall was added later, the top of the bank behind it being used as a wall-walk. There was a gate in the centre of each of the four walls, and where the main roads crossed in the middle of the fortress the headquarters building, the *principia,* was placed. Here the standards were

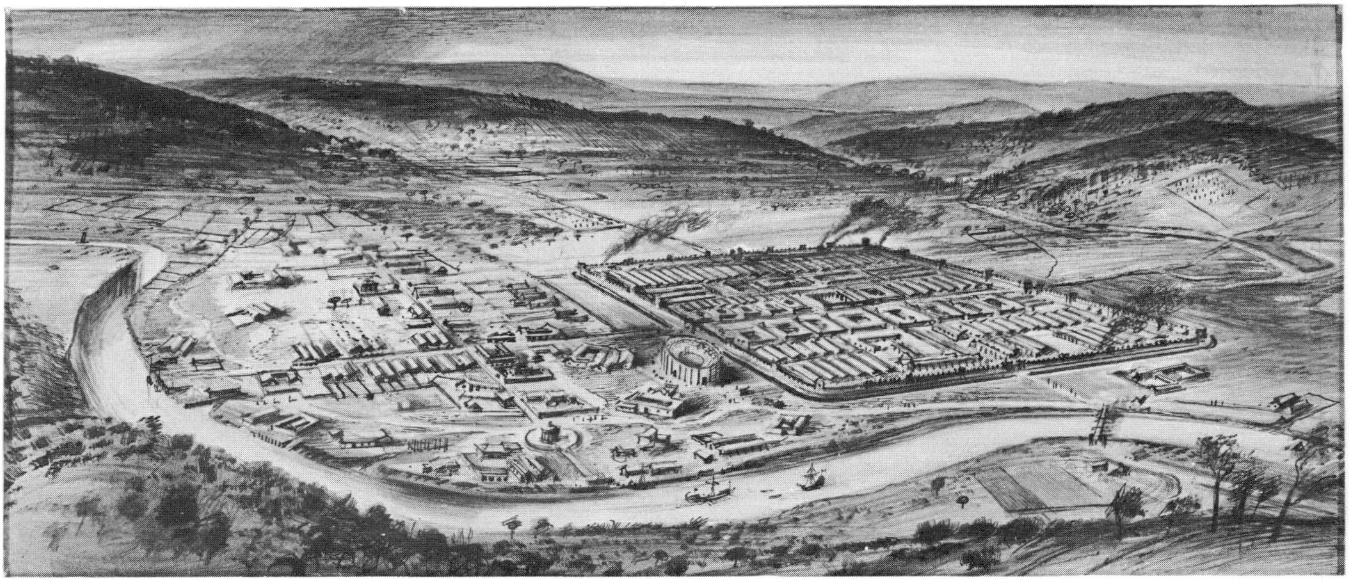

6. *The legionary fortress at Caerleon-on-Usk, Monmouthshire: This was the permanent base for the Second Augustan legion after Wales was conquered in A.D. 75.*

7. Inside the legionary fortress at Caerleon: On the right is the fortress wall with a sentry on the wall-walk behind the battlements: the turrets are look-out posts. On the left are the barracks with the verandah in front of the men's cubicles. Smoke is rising from the cook-houses at the back of the ramparts.

housed, the pay-chests and accounts were kept, and besides offices for the clerks there was a great hall with a dais for ceremonial and for courts-martial. Nearby the commanding officer, the Legate, had his house, and there were also private quarters for the staff officers, the tribunes and the camp-prefect. Other buildings were armouries, granaries and stores,

schools of instruction for the junior officers (the centurions), a hospital and a prison.

The soldiers lived and slept in long rows of barracks arranged in pairs facing inwards; each block held a unit of about 80 to 100 men, a century. Eight men shared two cubicles; they slept in the inner one, and kept their equipment in the outer room which opened on to a covered verandah. Their officers, a centurion and his deputy, had a set of larger rooms at one end of the barracks. For each unit there were separate cook-houses behind the fort rampart nearby. Soldiers' rations consisted of a measure of corn issued from the granaries, which was stone-ground, and the flour baked into bread or biscuits, lard or oil for cooking, and wine, often of poor quality.

In their leisure time, the soldiers went outside the fortress to

8. *The Governor and the subject people: The Governor addresses the people in the Forum of a new town. He is wearing a cuirass made of moulded pieces of bronze stitched to a leather jerkin, over this is draped a military cloak. The man on the left is wearing a hooded cloak, the* cucullus.

the amphitheatre (fig. 14), to the baths (fig. 17), to the temples (fig. 24), and to the little settlement of traders and residents that grew up outside the gates: here too, on the roads leading away into the country, were the military cemeteries with the tombstones on which was carved a soldier's portrait, and which recorded finally his name, rank, age and length of service.

THE SCHEME OF GOVERNMENT

Britain was now one of the provinces of the Roman Empire, and, like other lands from Spain to Roumania, under the rule of the Emperor living in Rome. He it was who appointed the Governor, who was responsible both for military and civil affairs, and the Procurator, who was responsible for money matters. The Governor was a person of good birth who had been

a member of the Senate at Rome, and a commander of a Legion (fig. 8). Such a one was Agricola, whom the Emperor Vespasian sent to Britain in A.D. 78; he not only led the legions himself on campaigns in Scotland, but started many improvements in civil life during his term of office. There had been a rebellion in A.D. 60-61, led by Boudicca (*Boadicea*), queen of the Iceni, the tribe who lived in what is modern Norfolk, which had caused much hardship and distress from which the people had barely recovered, and Agricola's reorganisation was very necessary.

Britain by nature is divided into two main parts, the lowlands of the south and east, the highlands of the west and north; a line drawn from the Exe to the Humber is approximately their boundary. The soils and the contour of the country in the lowland zone are better suited to habitation and cultivation, and consequently in early times this area was the more densely populated; it formed the civil zone of the province. In it towns were founded or grew up at junctions on the main roads (fig. 11); Roman-Britons built themselves fine houses or substantial farms (villas) in the Roman style on their estates in the country (fig. 28), and peasants continued to live in their farmsteads as in Cranborne Chase, Dorset, content with very little alteration in their way of life (fig. 16).

In the highland zone, where conquest had been slow and difficult, and the people were scattered, there was always a military occupation. The legions were quartered here in their fortresses on the fringe of the hills (figs. 6-7), whilst the auxilia were posted up-country in forts very similar in appearance and plan to the legionary base, but smaller (fig. 10). The forts were linked by a network of military roads, and so in the case of trouble in the highlands the auxiliaries could keep in touch with each other, and a detachment of legionaries could quickly come up to assist them. In the military zone, the Roman-Britons continued to live in their native farmsteads and settlements and were not encouraged to start town life with one or two exceptions. They paid their dues to the local military post.

In the civil zone, local government was organised in the towns, which had a Town Council (*Ordo*) with elected magistrates and other officials, modelled on the Roman pattern. The Council was responsible for collecting the taxes for the Procurator from the town and from the people in the surrounding countryside, as well as money to pay for their own affairs.

HADRIAN'S WALL

Once the Romans gave up the idea of conquering Scotland, they had to fix a frontier in the north. The Emperor Hadrian on his visit to Britain in A.D. 122 decided on a line across the narrowest part of the island from the mouth of the Tyne to the Solway Firth. Across the wild moors, for a distance of over 70 miles, Hadrian's Wall was built by the legionaries to be a sign to the barbarians of the northern limit of the Empire. It was built of stone, with a core of concreted rubble, 8 feet thick and 20 feet high, including a parapet which protected the patrols on the wall-walk; there was a ditch in front of it except where it crossed the crags. The line was carefully chosen to command a good look-out to the north (fig. 10).

The Wall was patrolled by auxiliaries, 50 of whom were quartered in each of the "milecastles", which were fortlets containing small double barracks attached to the back of the Wall at intervals of a Roman mile (fig. 9). Between the milecastles there were two

9. A milecastle on Hadrian's Wall: These small forts are spaced at intervals of one Roman mile along the Wall and are built on to its south side.

turrets with stairs to go up on the wall-walk. The rest of the garrison lived in the 19 large auxiliary forts close behind, or on the line of the Wall. To the south of the Wall was a road, the Military Way for moving troops and supplies. There was also another patrol

10. Hadrian's Wall at Housesteads, Northumberland: The Wall crosses the valley of the Knag Burn, where there was a gate to the north, and continues along the crags into the distance. There is a turret on the right with a soldier on the wall-walk finishing his patrol, and beyond the fort there is a milecastle in the distance. The troops are moving eastwards along the Military Way: the standard bearer is carrying the vexillum, *the ensign of the detachment.*

The fort is Housesteads; its Latin name was Vercovicium. *It housed nearly 1,000 auxiliaries in twelve barracks. The buildings in the centre of the fort are the headquarters building, the commandant's house, a hospital, workshops, granaries and stores. Outside the fort is a civil settlement where traders lived: there is a bath building for the soldiers beside the burn. The straight lines of the* Vallum *ditch and banks are on the left, marking the southern boundary of the military zone.*

line along the south side of an earthwork called the Vallum, a broad flat-bottomed ditch between two banks, which sealed off the military frontier works from the civil province.

The patrols could go out northwards through gates at the forts and milecastles to learn from the friendly tribes nearby of any threat from the distant barbarian. Hadrian's frontier system was a success; so much so that some twenty years later the line was advanced to take in the lowlands of Scotland. A turf rampart on a stone foundation and a ditch, known as the Antonine Wall from the reigning Emperior Antoninus Pius, was built across the narrow Forth-Clyde isthmus, together with the necessary forts and roads for the garrison. It lasted only a short time, from A.D. 143 to about 190, in the face of the gathering strength of the barbarians, and a withdrawal to Hadrian's line then had to be carried out. Thereafter Hadrian's Wall protected Britain from attacks from the north.

TOWNS AND TOWN LIFE

Before the conquest the Britons had lived together in large communities in their hill-forts, and so the practice of town life was not altogether new to them. Under Roman guidance they left the hilltops to settle on the lower ground alongside the new roads, often beside a river crossing but on firm ground above the flood level. The most important towns were those that took the place of the Celtic tribal centres, as is shown by their Latin names, such as *Isca Dumnoniorum* (Exeter), capital of the Dumnonii, the tribe that lived in Devon and Cornwall. In this way the centre of government in each district remained practically unchanged.

The size of each town was fixed ultimately by its defences, an earth rampart, later rebuilt as a stone wall, and a ditch. One of the largest was *Corinium* on the Cotswolds, now a town of much the same size, Cirencester; others, like that at Caerwent, Monmouthshire (fig. 11), were little larger than a modern village.

The shape of each town varied according to the site. The town was entered through gateways, which had main arches for wheeled traffic, and smaller ones for foot-ways (fig. 12). Along the main streets there were colonnades on the side-walk to protect people from the weather. The side streets were laid out to cross at right-angles, forming a sort of chess-board plan. In the streets were public fountains, from which people carried water to their houses.

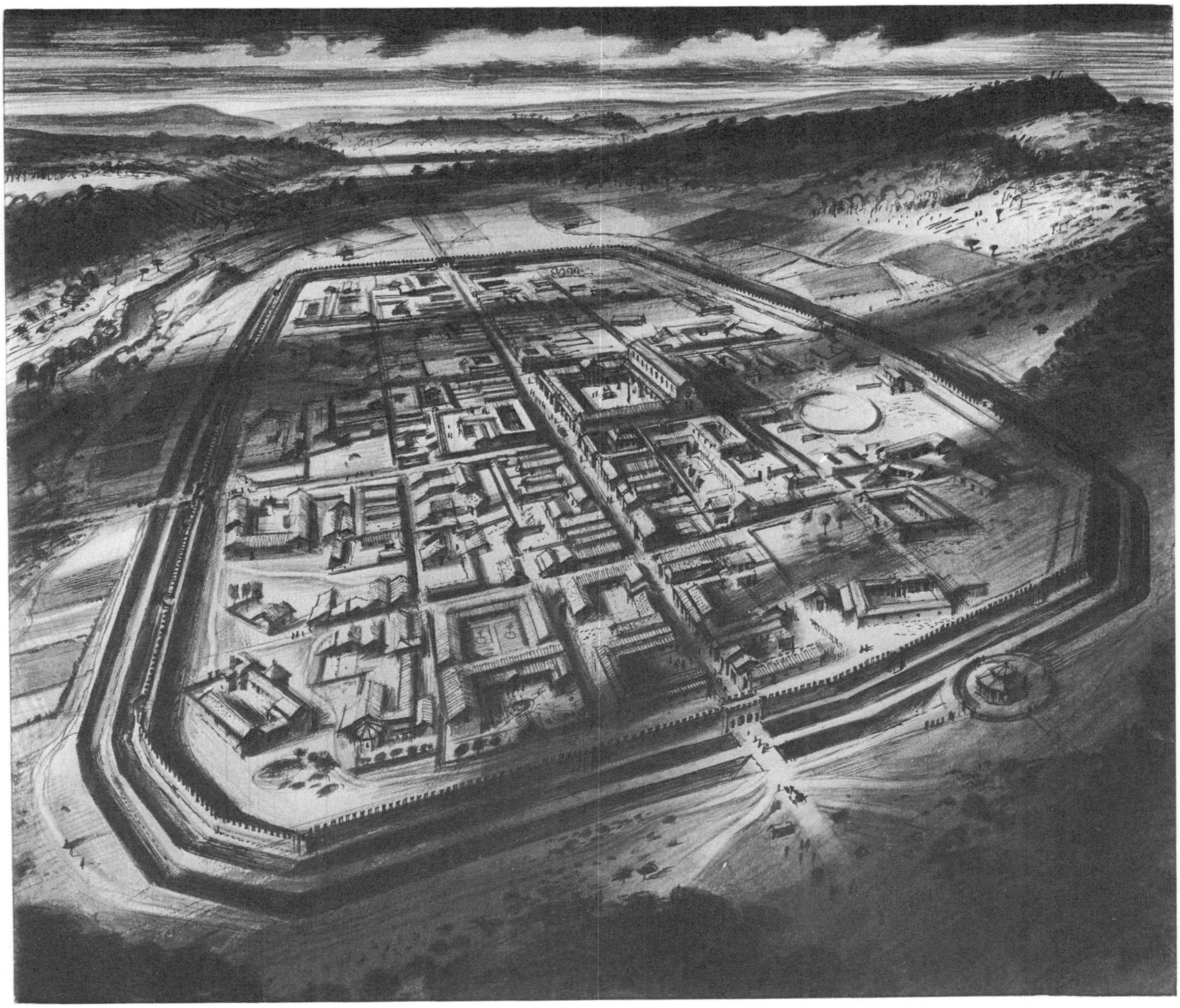

11. The Romano-British town at Caerwent, Monmouthshire, from the east: This town was founded for the Silures, the Celtic tribes in South Wales, after they had been conquered in A.D. 75-80. The main street ran east to west, and on it were sited the Public Baths, the Forum with the Basilica, a temple and many shops.

The chief public building, the Forum, stood in the centre of the town; it combined what today we should call the town hall, the law courts, the market and council offices. The citizen went in through an imposing entrance gateway into an open courtyard, the Forum proper, which had a colonnade along three sides with rows of shops and offices. Here the market was held and here the townspeople met to discuss their affairs, as in the great Forum in Rome. On the fourth side, opposite the entrance, was a lofty hall, the Basilica, where the Town Council met, and where the magistrates worked (fig. 8).

Nearby were the Public Baths (*Thermae*), where everyone went for relaxation in the afternoon. An outer court was used for athletics and ball games; inside the building there were undressing rooms, and then a series of spacious rooms heated by hot air from a furnace to different temperatures. The bather passed through three of these in turn, each a little hotter and moister, until he sweated as in Turkish Baths today, and on his return to the outermost room he finished off with a cold plunge in a sunk bath (fig. 17).

The shops in the town were quite small, more like stalls than a modern shop; some sold things like pottery, cutlery, and metalwork, others foodstuffs from the country, or wine or oil imported from the continent in tall handled jars called *amphorae* (fig. 22).

The houses were mostly single-storeyed (fig. 13). The largest had a central courtyard on to which a great number of rooms opened beneath a covered verandah; others, more modest, consisted of only five or six rooms opening on to a corridor that led in from the street at the side of the house. There were separate quarters for the slaves, who did all the cooking and housework and were the owner's personal attendants.

AMUSEMENTS

For amusement the townsfolk went to the amphitheatre to see the Games, which included bear-baiting, cock fights, wrestling and sometimes gladiatorial shows. Men armed with swords, spears, nets and firebrands fought against savage bears and other wild beasts caught and brought down from the highlands, or with each other, and the spectators staked their money on the contests.

12. *A street in Roman London, looking west towards Newgate: On the right is an inn, and a typical arcade of shops. Beyond the walls are tombstones alongside the road: the hills behind are Hampstead and Harrow.*

The amphitheatre was a big open-air oval building often placed for safety outside the town walls as at Cirencester or Dorchester. The people sat on tiers of wooden seats raised on an earth bank above the stone walled arena. There were special seats of honour for the magistrates and town councillors, one of whom had given a large sum of money to pay for the performance. On the day of the Games, which was a public holiday, sideshows might be set up outside the amphitheatre; there would be acrobats, jugglers and little booths which sold refreshments (fig. 14).

Theatres in which plays could be acted, are not common in Britain though there are plenty in Gaul. There was one at Canterbury (fig. 13) and another at St. Albans, (*Verulamium*), with a stage which had a slot into which a curtain could be lowered in the Roman fashion: it also had a place for beast-fights in front of the stage.

Chariot races were probably held in Britain on a course in the open. The drivers controlled a team of two or four ponies harnessed to the pole — a central shaft — of the light car; they drove them round an oval track, the circus, cornering very skilfully round the wooden bollards that marked the turning-points as depicted on a mosaic from Horkstow, Lincolnshire, in the British Museum.

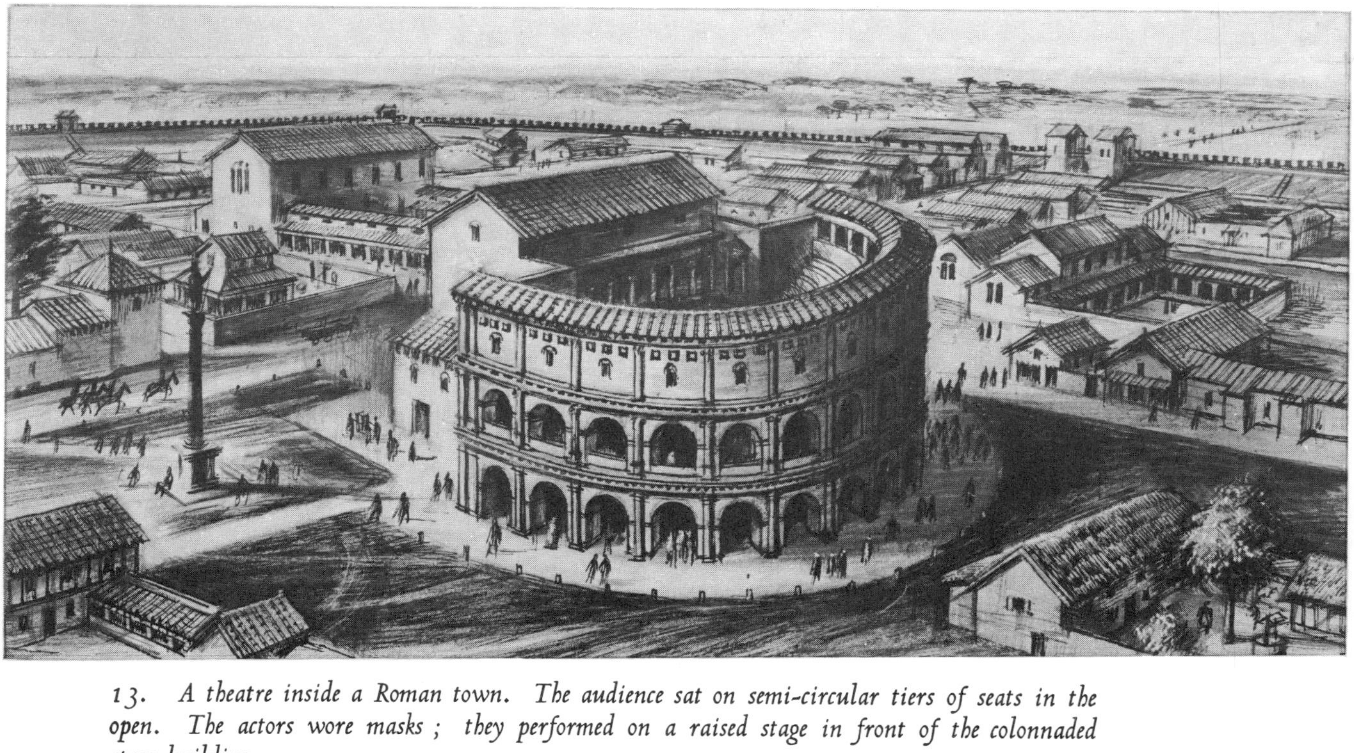

13. A theatre inside a Roman town. The audience sat on semi-circular tiers of seats in the open. The actors wore masks ; they performed on a raised stage in front of the colonnaded stage-building.

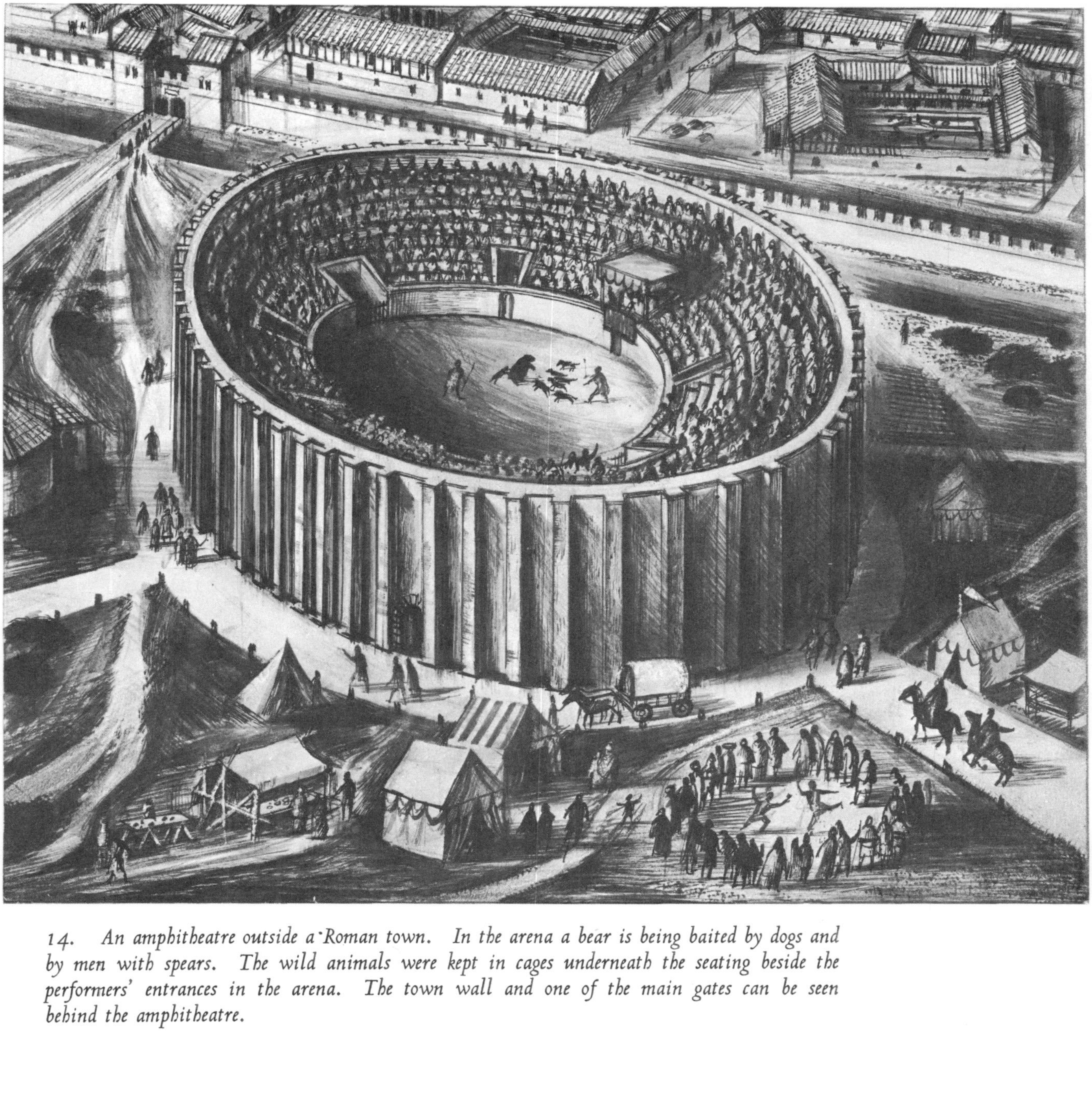

14. An amphitheatre outside a Roman town. In the arena a bear is being baited by dogs and by men with spears. The wild animals were kept in cages underneath the seating beside the performers' entrances in the arena. The town wall and one of the main gates can be seen behind the amphitheatre.

BUILDING CRAFTS AND TECHNIQUES

To build their towns, the Britons had to learn new techniques. The Roman surveyors and engineers showed them how to lay out straight streets and buildings at right angles; they learned from the masons how to work stone, to cut and tool it into rectangular blocks of even size for walling, to shape and set stones to form an arch supported on wooden centering, to hew a block to make a round column shaft, or to chisel a decorative pattern in relief, or to sculpture an image in the round.

They learned in what proportion to mix sand, lime and stone or tile chippings to make mortar or cement for floors, or concrete that would set firm in the core of a wall or form the vault of a large public building.

To keep buildings weather-tight, they learned to roof them with two sorts of heavy red tiles, which were manufactured from local clays; the *tegula,* a flat tile with upturned edges, and the *imbrex,* a semi-circular tile that covered the joins. To keep rooms warm, they learned how to lead hot air from a furnace under a floor raised on pillars of tiles and bedded on thick concrete (a hypocaust) and up the walls in box flue-tiles (fig. 15).

They were instructed how to bring pure water to public fountains in the towns in lead pipes or conduits, and how to drain the streets and buildings.

In two or three generations such things were part of general knowledge in Britain.

COUNTRY LIFE

Unlike the present day, more people lived in the country than in the towns in Roman Britain. The well-to-do built themselves new houses in the Roman style in pleasant places on their estates. These " villas " were country house and farm combined; the farm buildings, built of half-timber, were grouped round an enclosed courtyard, with the house placed along one side of it. In the largest villas like Bignor in Sussex, or Woodchester in Gloucestershire, the house was separate, built around an inner courtyard (fig. 27).

Most of the cultivated land grew wheat, spelt and barley. The small fields were tilled by a light wooden plough with an iron share pulled by two oxen yoked together. At harvest only the ears of corn were cut with iron sickles; they were threshed on a clay threshing-floor with wooden flails or trodden out by the oxen ; the grain was winnowed from the chaff by shaking it in a basket-cradle or by fanning. If it was damp, the grain

15. Building techniques: A Roman house, showing the heating system: a slave is stoking the furnace on the left, and the lady of the house is sitting in a basket chair in the heated room above the hypocaust. Any smoke could escape through the chimney vents at the top of the wall flues. The house is stone-built round a little courtyard and has a tiled roof. Above are: 1. Roof tiles, slates and nails. 2. A sculptured head. 3. Surveyor's and mason's tools: a set square, plummet, dividers, stone-hammer and chisel. 4. A barrel vault in brick and concrete with its timber supports. 5. A box flue-tile. The stamped patterns on the face gave a grip for the wall plaster.

16. Country life   a. Hunting the boar

would be dried at a low heat in a kiln with double floors, before it was stored in bins in the granaries or ground into a coarse flour, by slaves, in hand querns or at small water mills.

The animals reared were cattle, sheep and pigs; they were all smaller than those existing today. The sheep grazed free on the downland and were looked after by a shepherd. The wool was spun and woven on a handloom by the women and slaves in the house, and

b. A *Romano-British ploughman*

c. Harvesting

the lengths of cloth cleansed with fuller's earth to rid it of the grease. Some of it was made up into hooded woollen cloaks (fig. 16e) that were exported to other parts of the Empire.

Much of the land remained heath and forest in which wild deer, boars and even bears and wolves lurked. The Roman Britons hunted the wild animals with big dogs like an Irish wolfhound.

d. Threshing and winnowing

e. A Romano-British shepherd

DAILY LIFE

The Roman Briton rose at dawn and quickly dressed. Generally speaking men wore a tunic, cloak and sandals, the women a long dress girdled at the waist and a cloak which was wrapped around and fastened by a brooch. The ladies spent a long time at their toilet; one slave held the mirror for her mistress, another combed and pinned up her hair, while others brought her make-up and jewellery.

For the men, the morning was given over to work and business; letters were written on waxed boards with a bronze point called a *stylus*, and tied up and sealed (fig. 19). The afternoon was the leisure time. In the country a small suite of nicely decorated heated bathrooms in a wing of the house replaced the Public Baths of the towns (fig. 17).

The main meal of the day was taken in the evening. The dining-room (*triclinium*) was the largest and best room in the house; like the bath-rooms it was heated by hot air in a hypocaust under the floor. The walls and ceilings were decorated with panels of painted patterns, mostly stripes or floral designs.

The family and their guests reclined on three couches beside a low table arranged on three sides of a square and the slaves waited on them. Each person had a bowl or platter, usually made of a glossy red imported pottery called Samian ware, and a drinking cup; the best dishes were of silver. People ate with their fingers mostly, but they had special spoons to open and drain the oysters for which Britain was famed. When night fell, little oil-lamps were lit and placed on a bronze stand (fig. 20).

There was no carpet on the floor but instead there were patterns made up of different coloured cubes of stone set in cement, forming a mosaic, with a very pleasing effect. Most of the designs were geometric, but pictures of the gods and heroes, such as Orpheus playing his magic music to the animals, or scenes from the sad story of Aeneas and Queen Dido, could be seen in the houses of the well-to-do.

17. The Baths: The bathers in a country house are in the plunge-bath in the cold room (frigidarium) *after sweating in the hot rooms* (caldaria). *There is a mosaic floor with a pattern of fishes round the bath, which was lined with lead to make it watertight. The vaulted ceiling and walls are painted.*

18. *(Left) razor, oil-flask, nail-cleaner,* strigil *and comb ; (right) silver goblet, spoons and knives.*

MINING AND METAL WORKING

Mines in the Roman Empire were state property and were either under military control or leased to agents. The Romans mined some gold and copper in Wales, silver and lead chiefly in Derbyshire and on the Mendips, iron in Sussex and in the Forest of Dean, and tin in Cornwall. There was a good deal of surface working, but when necessary shafts or adits were dug to reach the metal-bearing seams. The underground galleries were kept dry by a system of water-wheels, which scooped the water up in buckets into a channel at a higher level. The miners were convicts or slaves; they used picks and wedges, and carried lamps (fig. 21).

The ores were carried up to the surface where they were crushed and then smelted in a furnace to extract the precious metals. In the case of lead, the silver was removed by a second smelting and cast into small ingots. The lead was then ladled into long rectangular wooden moulds, and before the metal cooled and hardened, the ingot stamped with the Emperor's or the agent's name. Lead ingots weighed about 150-200 pounds each.

Many metal articles of daily use were made locally in Britain. The smith in his leather apron, with his hammer and tongs, working at his anvil must have been a familiar figure in town and countryside (fig. 22). The Romano-Britons were fine craftsmen in bronze-work; their speciality was inlay in many coloured enamels, which they had started

19. *Wooden writing tablets, bronze* stylus *and pen, ink-pots and scroll.*

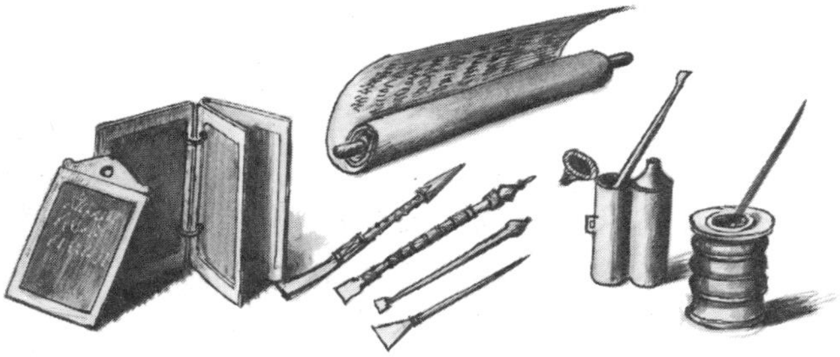

20. *The evening meal in the* triclinium.

21. *Mining: The convict miners are going down into the lead mine in charge of an overseer who is carrying a wrench: the first man holds a lamp, the others their picks and wedges. The lead ingot in the foreground is stamped with the name of the Emperor Hadrian. The small ingots are of silver and pewter, a mixture of tin and lead.*

to do before the Romans came. Unfortunately they rarely used their traditional flowing Celtic designs to ornament the new forms, but copied imported naturalistic work.

POTTERY MAKING

Every Romano-British household needed cooking vessels and table ware for everyday use. Some of the fine earthenware, like the glossy red Samian ware, as well as glass were luxuries imported from France and Germany, but the black and grey coarse pottery was made locally in Britain.

The potter's fields were, of course, on clay soil where the raw material was at hand, where there were springs for puddling the clay, and where there was plenty of wood available for stoking the kilns. The potteries in the New

22. *Smithing: The assistant holds a molten iron bar with tongs on the anvil ready for the smith to strike: the smith wears a leather apron to protect him from the sparks. Above the forge are finished tools, a chisel, pincers, tanged sickle and a knife.*

23. A Roman pottery kiln : Above are some of the different kinds of pots that were made in Britain. 1. Cordoned jar. 2. Bead-rim pot. These are both improved native British types made locally in the 1st century A.D. 3. Carinated bowl. 4. Jug. 5. Face-urn. 6. Cooking pot with everted rim. 7. Pie-dish decorated with scored lines. 8. Castor-ware cup with a hunting scene in relief. 9. A drinking-cup with white painted pattern. 10. Mortarium, a mixing bowl with gritted inside surface. 11. Flanged bowl of red colour-coated ware from the New Forest potteries. 12. Amphora for wine or oil, imported from France or Spain.

Forest and at Caistor on the river Nene in Northamptonshire are the best known of the British factories.

The potter shaped the vessel on his wheel, pressing the clay inwards to form the neck, outwards to shape the rim. Sometimes he stamped or incised a pattern on the damp clay, or when it had dried and hardened he dipped the pot in a ' slip ' of liquid clay to colour it. The pots were stacked one above the other in the upper part of the kiln, which was then closed by a dome of turf and brushwood. The furnace in the lower part of the kiln was lit and stoked and the draught forced the hot air along a flue and upwards through holes in the floor to bake the pottery. Sometimes a firing went wrong and the pots sagged or were discoloured; such " wasters " were thrown away. The perfect pots were sent away from the potteries to shops in the towns or taken by pedlars round the country, so that even the peasants in the hill country were able to buy a variety of mass-produced wares.

RELIGION

The Romans coming to Britain brought their gods and goddesses with them, Jupiter, Minerva, Mars, Diana and other deities. They also introduced the worship of the Emperor, and of personifications of abstract ideas like Victory or Fortune. But since all people in the Empire were free to choose which god they worshipped, Romano-Britons often continued to worship their own Celtic deities, though they now called them by a Latin name. For example, a Celtic war-god in the north of England, Cocid, was called Mars-Cocidius in the new style.

Each god had a separate temple built by his followers. Many Celtic gods were thought of as spirits belonging to a special place, so on hill-tops, or by a spring, small

24. A Romano-British sanctuary: The temple is in the middle of a walled enclosure in which there are also houses for the priest and for the pilgrims. The wooden hut beside the temple is a survival from an earlier shrine. Beside the gate is a booth where bronze votive offerings were sold.

25. The temple of Mithras, Walbrook, London : A pine cone is burning on the altar in front of the bull-killing relief. Two initiates wearing masks, one a raven (corax) *and one a lion* (leo) *are holding torches. The statues on either side are of Cautes and Cautopates, attendants on Mithras symbolising light and darkness by an upturned or downbent torch.*

square colonnaded temples were built to replace the old shrines (fig. 24). In the towns, the temples usually stood back from the streets in an enclosure (fig. 13).

Inside the temple the images of the god stood in a recess, and crowns, sceptres and other sacred things were kept there in safety. In the walled enclosures outside, the people gathered to take part in the festivals. Here inscribed stone altars were set up, often by people who had vowed to do so because they had received a favour from the god. Offerings of food and wine were made and animals were sacrificed; shrill pipes were played while each victim's throat was cut by the hooded priest. Afterwards there would be merry-making and a fair.

Some gods were gods of healing, like Sul-Minerva, a goddess who was associated with the hot springs at Bath, or Nodens, who had his temple and baths built inside an old hill-fort at Lydney, overlooking the Severn estuary, in Gloucestershire. To such places

26. *Roman galleys and a merchant ship entering a harbour adjoining a Saxon Shore fort. The naval galleys were propelled by banks of oars and were armed with sharp beaks for ramming.*

worshippers came to bathe, and often placed in the shrine a model bronze arm or leg to signify their need or to record their cure.

Mithras, the Persian hero-god, was worshipped in a special sort of underground temple (fig. 25); it had wide reclining benches at either side, and at the end a sculptured scene of Mithras killing a powerful bull, the flow of whose blood brought fertility to the earth. His followers had to undergo a succession of ordeals before they were

27. A signal tower on the Yorkshire coast, gives warning of the approach of the Saxon pirates in their long rowing boats. The smoke comes from burning pitch.

admitted to the sacred feast in the temple. There were seven stages of initiation, each grade with an appropriate name, like *Miles,* the soldier, or *Corax,* the Raven, and *Leo,* the Lion, taken from the magic animals in the story of Mithras. Many of the worshippers of Mithras were soldiers; women were not admitted to the sect.

There were Christians in Britain, and some, like Saint Alban, were martyred before the Emperor Constantine adopted the faith officially early in the fourth century A.D. They must have met mostly in private houses in rooms set apart and specially decorated, like the one at Lullingstone, Kent. Only one small town church has been discovered, at Silchester, although sacred symbols like the Chi-Rho, a monogram formed from the Greek initials of Christ, are often found incised on platters or spoons.

THE END OF ROMAN BRITAIN

For over two hundred years Britain prospered under Roman rule; life was comfortable, there was plenty to buy, it was easy to travel, there was peace and people felt secure. But

28. A villa attacked by barbarians: The people are fleeing carrying their possessions. The villa has two courtyards: the outer is the farmyard, with the barns, stables and a threshing floor; the inner is a formal garden, with the principal rooms of the owner's house on the near side and the slaves' quarters on the far side. The raiders have set fire to the bath suite.

on the continent, the Empire had more than once been invaded by barbarians from across the Rhine and the Danube. Now it was Britain's turn. From northern Germany and Denmark out of the mouths of the rivers Elbe and Weser came Saxon pirates in their long low rowing boats, to harry the Channel and North Sea coasts. From across the Irish Sea the Irish pirates in their skin boats (curraghs) came flocking to raid the western shores.

To meet this menace a new scheme for defence had to be devised; the army was reorganized and made more mobile, and a chain of forts was built along the coast from the Wash to Southampton Water, and some in Wales. These forts of the Saxon Shore were much smaller than a legionary fortress but they were very strong. They had one narrow gate, and high thick walls with projecting bastions on which heavy catapults were mounted to give flanking fire. Near each fort was a harbour, from which galleys of the British fleet could set out to engage or watch for the raiders, or protect the merchant ships (fig. 23). At Dover there were two lighthouses to guide them, one on each side of the harbour.

The pirates were not the only thing that troubled Britain in the fourth century; beyond the screen of friendly tribes on the northern frontier were the Picts, who had lately been joined by settlers from Northern Ireland, the Scots. Many times they crossed the Wall to raid together, and on one occasion in A.D. 367-8 they joined forces with the sea-borne Saxons and overwhelmed the army that was sent against them. In that year even the great country houses of the south were attacked and looted; the people fled or were carried off by the marauding bands of barbarians. Until the Emperor Valentinian was able to send reinforcements from Gaul under Count Theodosius, nowhere was safe.

As soon as peace was restored, a set of signal stations were built along the Yorkshire coast so that the fleet as well as the army at its headquarters at York should have good warning of another such invasion. Each post was like a little fort, with a wall with bastions at the angles, and a ditch, and in the centre the high signal tower stood overlooking the sea. If the Saxon ships were sighted, a message could be sent by flash or smoke by day, or by fire at night (fig. 27).

But although the barbarians were driven off that time, the days of peace in Roman Britain had come to an end; many owners did not go back to their villas, and country people thereafter had to live as best they could in a small way or go into towns for safety behind the walls. The towns too had their troubles; for many years they had not had enough money to keep up their standards, and buildings had fallen into decay. Nobody

cared if rubbish were dumped in the derelict theatre at St. Albans, or objected if carts were driven across the fallen columns of the Forum at Wroxeter.

At the end the Empire was in such straits that it was impossible to keep even a reduced army in Britain. While Alaric the Goth was preparing to march to attack Rome itself,

29. *Past and Present. (Above) the Roman-Britons bury their treasure. (Below) the archaeologists dig it up.*

the Emperor Honorius wrote in A.D. 409 a letter to the chief cities of Roman Britain and told them that henceforth they must look after themselves.

For some while Romano-British civilisation lingered on. In the towns the people patched up parts of ruined houses to live in, and they tried to make things locally for themselves. Since no more money came from the imperial mints they clipped pieces off their old coins for re-issue, or struck little slices from a bronze bar so small that fifty of them only cover the surface of a halfpenny. In troublous times, when the Saxons were approaching, people buried their money, their fine silver ware and other valuables in a hole in the floor or yard and fled; often the owners did not come back to dig the hoard up again, or the house was burnt down by the raiders and they could not find it. Gradually the Saxons pushed in and settled in the valleys. The Romano-Britons either fled westwards or sank into even greater poverty and slavery. The cities then fell into ruins; the red tile roofs collapsed, the mortar loosened in the walls, trees sprouted from the wall tops until in the end the ruins were swallowed up in undergrowth. Later the Normans and their successors routed amongst the debris for stone for their buildings, so that we know that the sites were not wholly forgotten through the ages.

PAST AND PRESENT

Today archaeologists go to such places to try and find out, by scientific excavation, as much as possible about the olden days. They systematically uncover the ruined walls, and so work out the plan of each building. They clear the soils off the floors, they dig beneath and collect the things that the Romano-British occupants lost or threw away. A study of a few small coins and some broken potsherds from beneath a floor may show the date at which the house was built. In so doing, the archaeologist may light upon the hoard of buried treasure concealed by the last inhabitant (fig. 29).

It is only by slow and careful work when digging, and by studying what is found scientifically, that the archaeologist has made it possible to write the story of Britain in Roman times long after the Romans had gone. The story is not finished yet because there is much more to find out about the past.